INDIAN
STORY AND SONG
FROM NORTH AMERICA

By

ALICE C. FLETCHER

AMS PRESS

NEW YORK

The Library of Congress cataloged this title as follows:

Fletcher, Alice Cunningham, 1845-1923.
    Indian story and song from North America. New York,
AMS Press [1970]
    xiv, 126 p.   22 cm.
    Includes music.
    Reprint of the 1900 ed.

    1. Folk-lore, Indian.   2. Indians of North America—Music.   I. Title.

E98.F6F6   1970   784.7'51   76-136396
ISBN 0-404-07880-X   MARC

Library of Congress   72

Reprinted from the edition of 1900, Boston
First AMS edition published in 1970

Manufactured in the United States of America

AMS PRESS, INC.
NEW YORK, N.Y.

To

MY INDIAN FRIENDS

FROM WHOM I HAVE GATHERED

STORY AND SONG

PREFACE.

At the Congress of Musicians held in connection with the Trans-Mississippi Exposition at Omaha in July, 1898, several essays upon the songs of the North American Indians were read, in illustration of which a number of Omaha Indians, for the first time, sang their native melodies to an audience largely composed of trained musicians.

This unique presentation not only demonstrated the scientific value of these aboriginal songs in the study of the development of music, but suggested their availability as themes, novel and characteristic, for the American composer. It was felt that this availability would be greater if the story, or the ceremony which gave rise to the song, could be known, so that, in developing the theme, all the movements might be consonant with the circumstances that had inspired the motive. In response to the expressed desire of many musicians, I have here given a number of songs in their matrix of story.

Material like that brought together in these pages has hitherto appeared only in scientific publications, where it has attracted the lively interest of specialists both in Europe and America. It is now offered in

vii

a more popular form, that the general public may share with the student the light shed by these untutored melodies upon the history of music; for these songs take us back to a stage of development antecedent to that in which culture music appeared among the ancients, and reveal to us something of the foundations upon which rests the art of music as we know it to-day.

Many of the stories and songs in this little book are now for the first time published. All have been gathered directly from the people, in their homes, or as I have listened to the earnest voice of the native priest explaining the ancient ceremonials of his fathers. The stories are close translations, losing only a certain picturesqueness and vigour in their foreign guise; but the melodies are exactly as sung by the Indians.

Indian myths embodying cosmic ideas have passages told in song, tribal legends have their milestones of song, folk-tales at dramatic points break into song; but into these rich fields I have not here entered. This collection reveals something of the wealth of musical and dramatic material that can be gleaned outside of myth, legend, and folk-lore among the natives of our country.

Aside from its scientific value, this music possesses

PREFACE

a charm of spontaneity that cannot fail to please those who would come near to nature and enjoy the expression of emotion untrammelled by the intellectual control of schools. These songs are like the wild flowers that have not yet come under the transforming hand of the gardener.

ALICE C. FLETCHER.

PEABODY MUSEUM,
HARVARD UNIVERSITY.

CONTENTS.

LIST OF SONGS.

LIST OF SONGS

INDIAN STORY AND SONG

STORY AND SONG OF THE
HE–DHU'–SHKA.*

It had been a warm September day; and I was resting in my hammock, swung from a wide-spreading tree that stood near the tent of my Indian host. We had partaken of our evening meal beside an outdoor fire. The mother was busy clearing away the supper dishes, the men had gone off to look after the horses, the children had fallen asleep, and I lay watching the shadowy darkness come out of the east and slowly pursue the glowing trail of the retreating sun, thinking of the Indian's imagery of night ever haunting and following upon the track of day, seeking to gain the mastery. I was aroused from my musings by hearing the mother say, "It is chilly!" for the fire had died down, and the deep blue of twilight was all about us.

She dropped beside the embers, blew them into a feeble blaze, threw on fresh wood, that crackled and sent up a shower of sparks and soon bright yellow flames illumined the under side of the branches beneath which I was swinging.

The call of the fire summoned one tall form after

* In the Indian words and vocables the vowels have the continental sound. *G* is hard, as in *go; dh* is like *th* in *the; th*, as in *thin; n* as in French *en.*

3

another out of the dusky surroundings, and around the blazing logs robes were spread here and there, on which the men reclined. By and by the women came and dropped down near the fire, and added the treble of their voices to the deep tones of the men, as the chat of the day's occurrences went on.

It was a peaceful, picturesque scene upon which I looked; and by very contrast my thoughts reverted to the preceding evening, when I had attended a meeting of the He-dhu'-shka, society composed of warriors. The gathering had been in a large tent; and, as the night was warm, the bottom of the tent cover had been lifted to let the breeze blow through. This had given an opportunity for the crowd outside to look within and watch the ceremony and the dramatic dance. To the right of the door, in two circles around the drum, sat the choir of men and women, all in their gala dress. Each member of the society, wrapped in his robe, with measured steps entered the tent, and silently took his seat on the ground against the wall. The ceremony had opened by the choir singing the ritual song which accompanied the act of charring the elder wood with which the face of the Leader was afterward to be painted. As memory brought back

4

the scene in vivid colours, — the blazing fire in the centre of the wide circle of muffled warriors, the solemn aspect of the Leader awaiting the preparation of the elder wood, and his strange appearance after the painting of his face, — I pondered wonderingly as to what it all might signify. In my perplexity I spoke from my hammock to one of the elder men in the group before me : —

"Grandfather, I wish you would explain to me the meaning of what I saw yesterday at the He-dhu′-shka Society. Tell me why the Leader put black on his face."

My friend was accustomed to my questionings, and all eyes were turned toward him as he replied :

"The Leader put the black cloud over his face, because the black cloud is worn by Thunder when it comes near to man. The song sung while this is being done tells that the Leader is making ready and impatiently awaits the commands of the approaching god of war." . . .

This is the song which accompanied the preparation and the putting on of the insignia of the thunder god. The music is expressive of the tremulous movement of the leaves, of the flying of the birds, of the stir of all nature before the advancing storm,

5

PUTTING ON THE INSIGNIA OF THE THUNDER GOD.

Omaha.   He-dhu'-shka.

Harmonized by Prof. J. C. Fillmore.

Mysteriously and with Agitation.

Non-g'dhe dhe-te hi-dha-ki-un te dhon-hi-de,

Non-g'dhe dhe-te hi-dha-ki-un te dhon-hi-de,

Non-g'dhe dhe-te hi-dha-ki-un te dhon-hi-de,

PUTTING ON THE INSIGNIA.

Non-g'dhe dhe-te hi-dha-hi-un te dhon-hi-de,

Non-g'dhe dhe-te hi-dha-ke-un te dhon-hi-de.

typifying the stirring of the heart of man when summoned to fight the enemies of his people.

At the close of the song and ceremony of blackening the Leader's face, I had seen the Leader take the pipe belonging to the society, fill it, and reverently lift the stem upward.

"When the Leader's face is painted," continued the old man, "he offers the pipe to Wa-ko*n*'-da (god). The words of the song then sung mean: Wa-ko*n*'-da, we offer this pipe (the symbol of our unity as a society). Accept it (and us). All the members must join in singing this prayer, and afterward all must smoke the pipe."

"The He-dhu'-shka Society is very old," continued my friend. "It is said to have been in existence at the time when the Omahas and the Ponkas were together as one tribe. There is a song with a dance which must be given at every meeting. It is to keep alive the memory of a battle that took place while we were migrating westward, and where defeat would have meant our extermination as a tribe. I will tell you the story.*

"One morning the tribe, whose country had been invaded by the Ponkas, made an unexpected assault

* The translation given is by my collaborator, Mr. Francis La Flesche.

8

PRAYER OF THE WARRIORS BEFORE SMOKING THE PIPE.

Omaha. He-dhu'-shka.

Harmonized by Prof. J. C. Fillmore.

Wa-kon-da dha - ni ga dhe ke, Wa-kon-da dha - ni

ga dhe ke, Wa - kon-da dha - ni ga dhe ke, E-

ha dha - ni hin ga *we dho he* *dho.*

upon the camp of the invaders. For a time it seemed as though the Ponkas would fare badly at the hands of their assailants, who were determined to drive out or destroy the intruders; but after a desperate struggle the Ponkas pushed their enemies back from the outskirts of the village, until finally their retreat became a rout. Both sides suffered great loss. The ground was strewn with the dead, and the grass stained with the blood of the warriors who fell in the battle; but the victory was with us, and we had conquered the right to dwell in that country.

"At the outset of the conflict a man bent with age emerged slowly from the door of one of the tents. The breezes played with his long white hair as he stood leaning on his staff, shading his face with one hand and looking intently in the direction whence came the noise of battle. As he recognised the voice of a warrior rushing to the fray, imitating as he ran the cry of some animal (his tutelary god), the aged man called after him:

" 'Once more! Once more be the undaunted warrior you have hitherto been! Utter aloud your mystic cry, and make the enemy to tremble with fear!'

"If a youth passed by, singing his death song, the old man would ask : —

" 'Who is that young man? He promises well.' Upon being told whose son he was, the aged man shouted: 'Ho-o! You have the spirit of your father. Be like him: turn not your face from the foe!'

"All day the old man stood at his door as though rooted to the ground. As the hours sped on, fainter and fainter grew the shouts and the cries of the contending men, until finally the sounds died away. Even then the venerable man moved not from his tent, but still stood watching. Lower and lower dropped the sun toward the western horizon, and all through the village anxious faces were turned in the direction whence the last sound of the fight had been heard. Suddenly a woman cried, —

" 'There they come!'

"At her words the old man leaned forward, straining his dim eyes to discern the distant figures on the far-off hill. In single file, on the warriors came, one preceding another, according to the grade of the honours he had won in the battle. The Herald hastened forth from the village to meet them and to learn their tidings. After a halt he turned and came on in advance of the men, shouting as he

came near the village the names of those who had
fallen in battle. As each name was called, the
wife or mother of the slain man rent the air with
sudden cry and wail, so that the whole village vi-
brated with the sound of sorrow as the victorious
warriors drew near. In the midst of all this com-
motion the aged watcher remained motionless, giving no sign of emotion as the wailing grew in volume, and stirring not even when he heard the names
of his two sons called in the long death-roll.

"As the warriors entered the village, the Herald
proclaimed the names of those who had distinguished
themselves in that memorable fight. Slowly the
men of valour approached their aged chief, who
bowed acknowledgment as each one spoke and laid
at his feet a trophy of war.

"Among the veterans came a young warrior, who,
in this his first battle, had, in a hand to hand con-
test, wrenched a club from the grasp of his antago-
nist, and had slain the enemy with his own weapon.
This club he presented to the old man, recounting
the deed. The chief, lifting the weapon, exclaimed
with a dramatic laugh: 'Ha, ha, ha! It is thus you
should treat your enemies, that they may fear you.
My exhortations to our young men have not fallen

on deaf ears. Those who sought to destroy our
people lie scattered and dead on the ground.
Wherever their shadows may wander, even there the
fear of you shall be. The enemy sought to make
me weep, but I laugh.' And the old man danced
to his triumphant laugh for the victory of that day.''

SONG OF THE LAUGH.

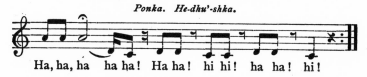

Ponka. He-dhu'-shka.

Ha, ha, ha ha ha! Ha ha! hi hi! ha ha! hi!

So this was the meaning of the monotonous song
that had accompanied the opening dance I had seen
at the He-dhu'-shka Society, where the dancer, with
body bent and with short rhythmic steps, had kept
time to the dramatic laugh of the song,—a song
that had seemed so aimless to me only the night
before.

''Every song of the Society has its story which
is the record of some deed or achievement of its
members,'' said another old man who was lying
beside the fire. ''I will tell you one that was
known to our great-great-grandfathers,'' and rising
upon his elbow he began:—

13

THE STORY AND SONG OF
ISH′–I–BUZ–ZHI.

"Long ago there lived an old Omaha Indian couple who had an only child, a son named Ish′-i-buz-zhi. From his birth he was peculiar. He did not play like the other children; and, as he grew older, he kept away from the boys of his own age, refusing to join in their sports or to hunt with them for small game. He was silent and reserved with every one but his mother and her friends. With them he chatted and was quite at ease. So queer a little boy could not escape ridicule. The people spoke of him as one 'having no sense,' and it seemed as though he would have no friends except his parents and a few women intimates of his mother.

"During the long winter evenings, when the old men who came to his father's lodge talked of bygone times and told tales of ancient heroes, this silent, seemingly heedless boy caught and treasured every word. He noted that the stories said that the mighty men of early days were armed only with clubs. He mused on this fact, and determined to make himself such a weapon. So he fashioned a four-sided club, practised with it in secret, and kept it constantly with him. He was well laughed at because he clung always to his club and would not learn the use of the bow; but he kept his own counsel, and, as the years went on, no one knew that the Sparrow-hawk had talked to him in a vision, and that he had become possessed of two of its sacred feathers.

"One day when Ish'-i-buz-zhi had grown to be a man, he heard a group of warriors discussing plans for an expedition against a tribal enemy. He determined to go with them; but he said nothing, and silently watched the men depart. That night he stole away and followed the trail of the warriors. In the morning one of the servants of the war party discovered him and reported to the Leader, who ordered that he be brought in. When the men saw that it was Ish'-i-buz-zhi, they joked him, and asked why he who cared only for the company of old women had come to them; but the Leader rebuked the warriors and received the youth kindly, and, when he found that the young man was not properly provided with clothing, bade his followers to fit him out from their own supplies. They obeyed, and they also made him a bow of ash and gave him some arrows.

"After many days' travel the party drew near to the enemy. A scout discovered their camp and reported having seen one of their men. At once the warriors prepared for battle, putting on the sacred paint and divesting themselves of unnecessary garments, which they handed over to Ish'-i-buz-zhi to take care of during the fight. But the young man had his own plans, and went to the Leader and asked permission to go and look at the enemy. With many cautions not to give an alarm and prevent surprise, the Leader consented, and off Ish'-i-buz-zhi started.

"Catching sight of the enemy, he threw away his bow, and, armed only with his club, rushed suddenly upon the foremost man, overthrew and killed him. When the war party came upon the scene, they saw with amazement what he had done, — how by the might of his single arm he had killed the Leader of the enemy and scattered his warriors.

"On the return of the Omaha men to their village the Herald, according to custom, proclaimed the deed of Ish'-i-buz-zhi. The old mother sitting in her tent heard his words, and called to her husband:

"'What is this that I hear? Go you out and learn the truth.'

16

" 'It is only their ridicule of our boy,' said the old man, loath to stir.

" The Herald cried again, and the old man arose and stood at the door of the tent. Then of a truth he learned that, single-handed, his son had vanquished the enemy. Again and again did Ish'-i-buz-zhi join war parties, and he was always the foremost to meet the enemy and to scatter them with his club.

"Many tales are told of him; for he was fond of joking, and was often absent-minded. It is said that his wife was skilled in embroidery, and would decorate his moccasins with fine porcupine quill work; and it disturbed her to see him put them on to go out of a morning when the dew was on the grass. So she took him to task for his thoughtlessness.

" 'While the grass is wet,' " said she, " 'carry your moccasins in your belt.'

"He obeyed; but he forgot to put them on when the grass was dry, and came home with feet bruised and sore, and his moccasins still in his belt.

"But these peculiarities no longer provoked ridicule, as when Ish'-i-buz-zhi was a boy; for as a man, generous and strong, he was beloved by the people.

17

DANCE SONG. (ICHIBUZZHI.)

Omaha. He-dhu-shka.

Harmonized by PROF. J. C. FILLMORE.

DANCE SONG.

The child who had feasted on tales of the old heroes had in his manhood reproduced their brave deeds. So it came to pass that, when danger threatened, it was to him that the people ran for help; and he never failed them."

The song refers to one of these appeals. An alarm arose, and to Ish'-i-buz-zhi, sitting in his tent, the people cried, "The enemy comes and calls for you, Ish'-i-buz-zhi."

STORY AND SONG OF THE LEADER.

AFTER many years of warfare the Omaha tribe made peace with the Sioux. One bright autumn day it was suggested that, in order to show their friendly feeling, a party of Omahas should visit the Sioux tribe. So the men and women made everything ready for the long journey.

Tent covers and camp belongings were fastened on trailing travaux, ponies were laden with gayly painted parfleche packs, containing the fine garments of the people and the gifts to be presented to the Sioux. Soon the motley-coloured line could be seen winding over the rolling prairie. The young men, mounted on their spirited horses, dashed off, racing with each other to attract the attention of the maidens, who could only follow with their eyes, so closely guarded were they by the elder women. Old men jogged along in groups, talking to each other, their lariats dragging through the grass, now and then snapping off the head of a wild flower or catching in a tangle of weeds. Boys made the air ring with their laughter, as they slipped off their ponies to shoot their small arrows at some imaginary game. It was a scene full of careless pleasure and happy movement under a cloudless sky.

When nearing the Sioux village, the people paused beside a stream to wash off the dust of travel, to put on their gayest attire, and to newly paint their hair and faces. The prairie was their vast dressing-room, and friendly eyes were their mirrors. Young men decked each other, and girls slyly put on touches of finery. Every one was moving about and busy, from the oldest man to the youngster captured from play to be washed and painted. At last the transformation was complete, from the dun, every-day colour to the brilliant hues of a gala time. Now messengers were despatched with small bunches of tobacco, tied up in bits of bladder skin (in lieu of visiting cards), to give notice of the visiting party's approach.

Suddenly some one asked, "What if the Sioux do not believe we are coming in peace, and should capture our messengers and attack us as we come near with our women and children?"

Such a reception had not before been thought of; and silence fell upon the people as they halted, under the gloom of the apprehension. At length the Leader stood up and said, — "We have made peace, we have come in good faith, we will go forward, and Wa-ko*n*'-da shall decide the issue."

STORY AND SONG OF THE LEADER

Then he struck up this song and led the way; and, as the men and women followed, they caught the tune, and all sang it as they came near the Sioux village.

In the words the Leader, as representing the Omahas, speaks: "I am advancing. I am moving toward you. Behold me, young men, warriors of the Sioux! Here I stand. Wa-kon'-da alone decides the destinies of men."

The visitors met with a welcome, and the breach between the two tribes was healed for many a long day.

SONG OF THE LEADER. A REST SONG.

Omaha. He-dhu'-shka.

Martial. M. M. ♩. = 63.

mf

Shu-b'dhe adhin-he on-don-ba i ga ho. . . . . . . Shu-

Ped.   ✳ *Ped.*

b'dhe adhin-he on-don-ba i ga ho. . . . . Sha-

✳ *Ped.*

With Spirit.

on-zhin-ga ha, dha-dhu anon-zhin on-don-ba ga,

f   *ff*

With Solemnity.

he. . . . . Wa-kon-da hi-dhe-g'dhon

✳ *Ped.*

SONG OF THE LEADER.

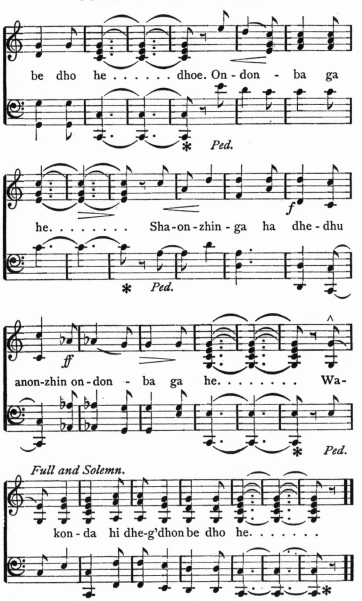

THE OMAHA TRIBAL PRAYER.

ACCORDING to the Omaha idea, a child during its infancy had no recognised existence as an individual or distinct member of the tribe, but remained as a part of its parents. When it could walk alone, at about three years of age, it was initiated into the tribal organisation through certain religious rites; but its responsible and individual life did not begin until its mind had "become white," as the Indians say. This expression referred to the dawn, to the passing of night into day, and represented the coming of the child out of the period where nothing was clearly apprehended into a time when he could readily recall past events with their distinctness of detail. This seeming mastery of the minutiæ of passing occurrences indicated that a stage of growth had been reached where the youth could be inducted into the religious mysteries through a distinct personal experience acquired in the rite, Non'-zhin-zhon, — a rite which brought him into what was believed to be direct communication with the supernatural powers.

In preparation for this rite the Omaha youth was taught the Tribal Prayer. He was to sing it during the four nights and days of his vigil in some lonely place. As he left his home, his parents put clay on his head; and, to teach him self-control, they placed a bow and arrows in his hand, with the injunction not to use them during his long fast, no matter how great the temptation might be. He was bidden to weep as he sang the prayer, and to wipe his tears with the palms of his hands, to lift his wet hands to heaven, and then lay them on the earth. With these instructions the youth departed, to enter upon the trial of his endurance. When at last he fell into a sleep or trance, and the vision came, of bird, or beast, or cloud, bringing with it a cadence, this song became ever after the medium of communication between the man and the mysterious power typified in his vision; and by it he summoned help and strength in the hour of his need.

In this manner all mystery songs originated, — the songs sung when healing plants were gathered and when the medicine was administered; when a man set his traps or hunted for game; when he desired to look into the future or sought supernatural guidance, or deliverance from impending danger.

The Tribal Prayer was called in the Omaha tongue Wa-kon'-da gi-kon: Wa-kon'-da, the power which could make or bring to pass; gi-ko*n*, to weep from conscious insufficiency, or the longing for something that could bring happiness or prosperity. The words of the prayer, Wa-ko*n'*-da dhe-dhu wah-pa'-dhi*n* a-to*n'*-he, literally rendered, are, Wa-ko*n'*-da, here needy he stands; and I am he.

This prayer is very old. Its supplicating cadences echoed through the forests of this land long before our race had touched its shores, voicing a cry recognised by every human heart.

THE OMAHA TRIBAL PRAYER.

Harmonized by PROF. J. C. FILLMORE.

Slow. Grave. Solemn.

Wa-kon-da   dhe - dhu   Wa-pa dhin   a - ton - he.

Con Ped.

Wa-kon-da   dhe - dhu   Wa-pa-dhin   a - ton - he.

Ped.

STORY AND SONG OF THE BIRD'S NEST.*

SCATTERED through an elaborate ritual and relig-ious ceremony of the Pawnee tribe are little parables in which some natural scene or occurrence serves as a teaching to guide man in his daily life. The following is an example.

The words of the song ("the sound of the young") are purposely few, so as to guard the full meaning from the careless and to enable the priest to hold the interpretation as a part of his sacred treasure. They are sufficient, however, to attract the attention of the thoughtful; and such a one who desired to know the teaching of the sacred song could first perform certain initiatory rites and then learn its full meaning from the priest.

"One day a man whose mind was open to the teaching of the gods wandered on the prairie. As he walked, his eyes upon the ground, he spied a bird's nest hidden in the grass, and arrested his feet just in time to prevent stepping on it. He paused to look at the little nest tucked away so snug

---

* An old priest of the rite gave me the story and song through Mr. James R. Murie, an educated Pawnee, and they are here for the first time made public.

and warm, and noted that it held six eggs, and that
a peeping sound came from some of them. While
he watched, one moved; and soon a tiny bill pushed
through the shell, uttering a shrill cry. At once
the parent birds answered, and he looked up to see
where they were. They were not far off, and were
flying about in search of food, chirping the while to
each other and now calling to the little one in the
nest.

"The homely scene stirred the heart and the
thoughts of the man, as he stood there under the
clear sky, glancing upward toward the old birds and
then down at the helpless young in the nest at his
feet. As he looked, he thought of his people, who
were so often careless and thoughtless of their children's needs; and his mind brooded over the matter.
After many days he desired to see the nest again.
So he went to the place where he had found it; and
there it was, as safe as when he left it. But a
change had taken place. It was now full to over-
flowing with little birds, who were stretching their
wings, balancing on their small legs, and making
ready to fly ; while the parents with encouraging
calls were coaxing the fledglings to venture forth.

"'Ah!' said the man, 'if my people would only

learn of the birds, and, like them, care for their young and provide for their future, homes would be full and happy, and our tribe be strong and prosperous.

"When this man became a priest, he told the story of the bird's nest and sang its song; and so it has come down to us from the days of our fathers."

SONG OF THE BIRD'S NEST.

Pawnee.

Transcribed from Graphophone and harmonized by EDWIN S. TRACY.

A TRYSTING LOVE-SONG.

ONE of the few delights of life in camp is the
opportunity the tent affords of ready access to the
open air. There is no traversing of stairways, no
crossing of halls, and no opening of reluctant doors,
but only the parting of the canvas, and our world is
as wide as the horizon and high as the heavens.
Even when the tent door-flap is snugly closed,
nature is not wholly shut out. Often I have lain
looking up at the stars as they passed slowly across
the central opening, and listened to the flight of the
birds as they travelled northward at the coming of
spring. And I have watched the birth of many a
day, from the first quivering primrose hue to the
full flush and glow of rosy colour, and then the stirring breeze, the waking leaves, and the call of the
birds breaking into song.

One morning I rose from my blankets and stepped
out under the broad dome of the sky, while all about
me in their shadowy tents the people slept. I wandered toward a glen, down which the water from a
little spring hurried to the brook. As I sat among
the fresh undergrowth, I watched the stars grow dim
and the thin line of smoke rise from the tents, tell-

ing that the mother had risen to blow the embers to a blaze and to put another stick or two upon the fire.

As I sat, thinking a multitude of thoughts, I heard a rustling upon the hill opposite me. Then there was silence, quickly broken by movements in another direction; while from the hill came the clear voice of a young man singing. In a moment more two women, whom I recognised as aunt and niece, appeared at the spring, the one elderly, the other young and pretty; but the singer was still invisible. The cadences of the song were blithe and glad, like the birds and the breezes laden with summer fragrance. The words, "I see them coming!" carried a double meaning. The girl for whom he had waited was in truth coming, but to the singer was also coming the delight of growing love and abundant hope.

The women filled their water vessels. The elder took no note of the song, but turned steadily toward the home path. The eyes of the maiden had been slyly searching the hillside as she slowly neared the spring and dipped up the sparkling water. Now, as the aunt walked away, the song ceased; and a light rustling followed, as the lover, bounding down the hill, leaped the brook and was

TRYSTING LOVE SONG.

Omaha.

Harmonized by **Prof. J. C. Fillmore.**

Light and Flowingly.

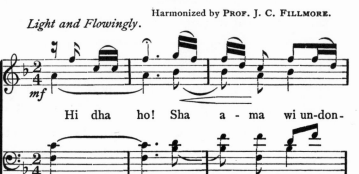

Hi dha ho! Sha a - ma wi un-don-

be a - me dho he, Sha a - ma wi un-don-

be a - me dho he Sha a - ma wi un-don-

be a - me dho he dhoe. Hi dha ho! Sha

*   Ped.

a - ma wi un-don - be a - me dho he. Sha

*   Ped.

a - ma wi un-don - be a - me dho he.

at the side of the girl. A few hasty words, a call from the aunt, a lingering parting, and I was alone again. The brook went babbling on, but telling no tales, the birds were busy with their own affairs, and the sunbeams winked brightly through the leaves. The little rift, giving a glimpse of the inner life of two souls, had closed and left no outward sign; and yet the difference!

There was a measured thud upon the trail, and an old woman with stooping shoulders passed down the glen. As she bent over the spring and took her water supply, I heard the young man's voice in the distance, singing his song as he wended his way home. The old woman heard it, too. She straightened up and looked steadily in the direction of the singer, slowly shook her head, picked up her water vessel, and turned away, her crooked figure disappearing in the shadows. Then I arose and followed the singer, trying to forget the warning shake of the old woman's head.

STORY AND SONG OF THE DEATH-
LESS VOICE.*

ORIGIN OF THE MA-WA'-DA-NI SOCIETY.

A LONG, long time ago a large number of warriors, under the leadership of a man noted through-
out the warlike tribes for his valorous deeds, started
forth to harass and, if possible, to drive a powerful
people from a territory which abounded in game.
This war party was out many days, had many a
weary march in search of the enemy, scouring the
country far and wide, keeping their scouts in the
front, rear, and flank; for the leader was determined
not to return to his village without the trophies of
war.

They came one day to a large grove with a clear
brook running through it. Here the Leader ordered
the camp to be pitched, that his little army might
rest awhile and repair their moccasins and clothing.
Sentinels were stationed so as to guard against
surprise. Hunters were sent forth, and returned
laden with game.

Night came on. There was no moon; and it was
dark, although the stars shone brightly. A fire

* The translation of the story is by Mr. Francis La Flesche.

blazed in the open air, and the men whose duty it was to dress and cook the meat, were moving about the burning logs; while others sat mending their moccasins by the firelight, listening to stories of battles, marvellous escapes, and strange adventures.

Supper was cooked, and the meat was piled on freshly cut grass spread upon the ground; and near by were set the pots of broth and the wooden bowls and horn spoons. The Leader was called to perform the usual sacred rites observed before the serving of food; and all the warriors gathered around the fire, each one eager for his portion of the meal. At a signal from the Leader every man bowed his head, and there was silence. Not a breath of air was stirring. Now and then could be heard the far-off dismal howl of the grey wolf or the cry of a strange bird startled from its nest by a coyote. Save from these and the crackling of the fire there was stillness in all the surroundings. The warriors had made their silent petitions to Wako*n'*-da, the power that moves all things. The Leader lifted his head. Then from the pile of meat he took a bit and raised it toward the sky, as an offering to that mysterious power, when suddenly the stillness was broken and the ceremony interrupted by a clear voice bursting into song, the echoes in the hills and valleys catching and repeating the strain.

Each warrior involuntarily grasped his bow. The Leader, ever keen and alert, exclaimed in a hoarse whisper, "The fire! the fire!" Immediately many hands were rubbing the flaming wood into the earth. Commands were hastily given by the Leader; and the warriors, with palpitating hearts, started out to form a ring around the spot whence the thrilling sounds came. The voice sang on. The ring grew smaller and smaller until in an open space the shadowy form of a tree loomed up before the advancing warriors. No escape was now possible for the singer, yet the song went on without hesitancy. The tree was now clearly visible. The song came to a close, and the echo died away in the distance. The men kept on toward the tree, with bows drawn and arrows strung. No form was seen running around inside the ring, seeking an opening for escape; but, lo! at the foot of the tree lay scattered the whitened bones and the grinning skull of a man. Death had claimed the body of this warrior and compelled its return to dust, but had failed to silence the voice of the man who, when living, had often defied death.

SONG OF THE DEATHLESS VOICE.

Dakota.

Majestic and Martial. Harmonized by EDWIN S. TRACY.

Hi dho ho... hi.. dho ho i dho hi

dho.. ha..... ha i dha. ah hi dha

ha hi dha ha. hi dha ha idha ha..

ha hi dho i dha he... e.... dho i.

SONG OF THE DEATHLESS VOICE.

Ah hi dho hi dho hi .. dho ho i dha i

dho . . . ha ha i dha

ah hi .. dha ha i dha ha . . . . hi dha ha i-

dha ha ha hi dha e dho he . . . dho.

INDIAN STORY AND SONG

The Leader, looking around upon his followers, lifted his voice and said:—

"This was a warrior, who died the death of a warrior. There was joy in his voice!"

The men to whom the strange experience narrated in this story came, afterward banded themselves together in order the better to serve their people, to present to the young men of the tribe an example of generosity in time of peace and of steadfast valour on the field of battle. They kept together during their lives and added to their number, so that the society they formed continued to exist through generations.

The story and song which has been handed down through all these years as the inspiration of the founders of the Ma-wa'-da-ni Society, embodies a truth honoured among all peoples,— that death cannot silence the voice of one who confronts danger with unflinching courage, giving his life in the defence of those dependent upon his prowess. Such a man might fall in the trackless wilderness, and his bones lie unhonoured and unburied until they blanched with age: still his voice would ring out in the solitude until its message of courage and joy should find an echo in the heart of the living.

STORY AND SONG OF *ZON–ZI'–MON–DE.*

VICTORY songs, of which this is one, were sung when the people with rhythmic steps celebrated ceremonially the return of victorious warriors. Because of its peculiar accessory, the scalp, this ceremony has been called by us the "scalp dance," although no Indian so designates it.

The contrast between the sentiment of this story, teaching respect and honour to the old, and the ceremony, as we baldly see it, is startling. But it is with the Indian as with ourselves: the cruelties of war and the gentler emotions are often intertwined, the latter surviving and lifting up a standard for emulation, the former passing away, dying with the instigating passion. Among the many hundreds of Indian songs I have known, none commemorate acts of cruelty.

Years ago the Omaha tribe and the Sioux met while searching for a buffalo herd; and, as was usual, a battle ensued, for each tribe was determined to drive the other from the region of the game. Although the Sioux outnumbered the Omaha, the latter remained victors of the field.

An old Omaha, interested to observe how some of

ZON-ZI-MON-DE.

Omaha.

Harmonized by PROF. J. C. FILLMORE.

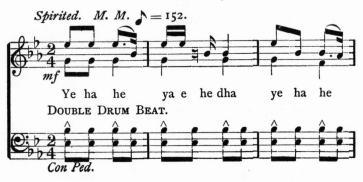

Ye ha he   ya e he dha   ye ha he

DOUBLE DRUM BEAT.

Con Ped.

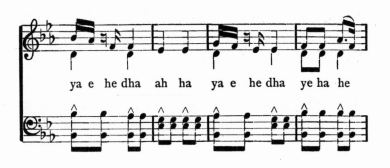

ya e he dha   ah ha   ya e he dha   ye ha he

ya e he dha   dha ha dhoe.   Zon - zi - mon-de

ZON-ZI-MON-DE.

a - ma sha e dhe.   Ah ha   ya e   he dha

e ha   he   ya e ha dha   dha ha dho.

the tribe would conduct themselves in their first battle, made his way toward the scene of conflict. It chanced that just as a Sioux warrior had fallen, pierced by an arrow, and the Omaha men were rushing forward to secure their war honours, this old man was discovered coming up the hill, aided by his bow, which he used as a staff   One of the young warriors called to his companions : —

"Hold! Yonder comes Zon-zi'-mon-de, let us give him the honours."

Then, out of courtesy to the veteran, each young warrior paused and stepped aside, while the old man, all out of breath, hastened to the fallen foe. There he turned and thanked the young men for permitting him, whom age had brought to the edge of the grave, to count yet one more honour as a warrior.*

The words of the song give the exclamation of the generous youth : "Zon-zi'-mon-de comes! Stand aside! He comes."

* To be the first to touch the body of an enemy counts as a war honour.

AN OMAHA LOVE–SONG.

THE words of many love-songs refer to the dawn, the time of the day when they are usually sung; but this reference is not a literal one. It figures the dawn of love in the breast of the singer. The Indian stands so close to Nature that he sees his own moods reflected or interpreted in hers.

The Indian words of this song, freely translated, are: —

> As the day comes forth from night,
>   So I come forth to seek thee.
> Lift thine eyes and behold him
>   Who comes with the day to thee.

Miss Edna Dean Proctor has rendered into charming verse the scene and the feeling of the hour, giving us an Indian love-song in its entirety. By her courtesy I am able to reproduce here her poem written some years ago, on hearing the melody which I had then recently transcribed during one of my sojourns among the Omaha Indians: —

> Fades the star of morning,
>   West winds gently blow,
> Soft the pine-trees murmur,
>   Soft the waters flow.

49

LOVE SONG.

Omaha.

Harmonized by PROF. J. C. FILLMORE.

LOVE SONG.

INDIAN STORY AND SONG

Lift thine eyes, my maiden,
　To the hill-top nigh,
Night and gloom will vanish
　When the pale stars die;
Lift thine eyes, my maiden,
　Hear thy lover's cry!

From my tent I wander,
　Seeking only thee,
As the day from darkness
　Comes for stream and tree.
Lift thine eyes, my maiden,
　To the hill-top nigh;
Lo! the dawn is breaking,
　Rosy beams the sky;
Lift thine eyes, my maiden,
　Hear thy lover's cry!

Lonely is our valley,
　Though the month is May;
Come and be my moonlight,
　I will be thy day!
Lift thine eyes, my maiden,
　Oh, behold me nigh!
Now the sun is rising,
　Now the shadows fly;
Lift thine eyes, my maiden,
　Hear thy lover's cry!

THE STORY AND SONG OF THE WREN.*

THIS little parable occurs in the ritual of a religious ceremony of the Pawnee tribe. The song has no words, except a term for wren, the vocables being intended only to imitate the notes of the bird, nevertheless, one can trace, through the variation and repetition of the musical motive, the movement of the gentle thoughts of the teacher as given in the story which belongs to the song.

"A priest went forth in the early dawn. The sky was clear. The grass and wild flowers waved in the breeze that rose as the sun threw its first beams over the earth. Birds of all kinds vied with each other, as they sang their joy on that beautiful morning. The priest stood listening. Suddenly, off at one side, he heard a trill that rose higher and clearer than all the rest. He moved toward the place whence the song came, that he might see what manner of bird it was that could send farther than all the others its happy, laughing notes. As he came near, he beheld a tiny brown bird with open bill, the feathers on its throat rippling with the fervour of its song. It was the wren, the smallest, the least

* Both story and song were recited to me by an old priest of the rite, and were interpreted by Mr. James R. Murie.

SONG OF THE WREN.

Pawnee.

Transcribed from Graphophone and harmonized by EDWIN S. TRACY.

Flowingly and Lightly.

mf

Ke-chi ra - ku - wa-ku whe ke re re we chi,

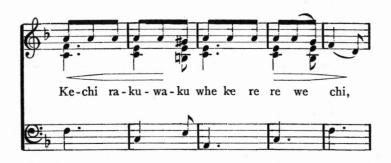

Ke-chi ra - ku - wa - ku whe ke re re we chi,

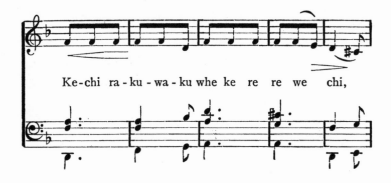

Ke-chi ra - ku - wa - ku whe ke re re we chi,

SONG OF THE WREN.

p

Ke - chi ra - ku - wa - ku whe ke re re we chi,

mf

Ke - chi ra - ku - wa - ku whe ke re re we chi,

Ke - chi ra - ku - wa - ku whe ke re re we chi.

powerful of birds, that seemed to be most glad and to pour out in ringing melody to the rising sun its delight in life.

"As the priest looked, he thought: 'Here is a teaching for my people. Every one can be happy, even the most insignificant can have his song of thanks.'

"So he made the story of the wren and sang it; and it has been handed down from that day,—a day so long ago no man can remember the time."

THE OMAHA FUNERAL SONG.

THERE was but one funeral song in the Omaha tribe, and this was only sung to honour some man or woman who had been greatly respected by the people.

What one would see, when this song was sung, was in violent contrast to the character of the music. The blithe major strains suggest only happiness. They hardly touch ground, so to speak, but keep their flight up where the birds are flitting about in the sunshine; and, if there are clouds in the blue sky, they are soft and fleecy, and cast no shadows. Yet the men who sang this song were ranged in line before the tent where the dead lay ready for burial. They had drawn the stem of a willow branch through a loop of flesh cut on their left arm, and their blood dripped upon the green leaves and fell in drops to the ground.

The meaning of this strange spectacle and its musical accompaniment, so apparently out of keeping, must be sought for in the beliefs of the people. It was a drama touching two worlds.

The shedding of blood was to express how vital was the loss. This act, visible to the mourners, was

SONG TO THE SPIRIT.

Omaha.

Harmonized by Prof. J. C. Fillmore.

Smoothly, with Tender Feeling.

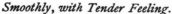

E   a   dha   ah   E   he   a   ha

Light beats on willow sticks.   No drums.

Peds. *f* and *p*.   ❋   *Ped.*

ah, he ah   E dha   ah   he a ha   ah

❋ *Ped.*

E dha ah E   ah E ah ha   e ha o   E dha

❋ *Ped.*

SONG TO THE SPIRIT.

he   he   dhoe ha   o   o   E   dha

Ped.

ha   he a ha   ah   E dha ah e

Ped.

ah E ah ha   e ha o   E dha he dho.

Ped.

an exhibition of sympathy; but music had power to reach the unseen world, so the song was for the spirit of the dead, who could not see the lacerated singers, but could hear them, as they sang to cheer him as he went forth, forced by death to leave all who were dear to him.*

The song was always sung in unison. The rhythm was accented by each singer beating together two small willow sticks.

There are no words to the song, only vocables; and these belong to the breathing or sighing class, indicative of emotion.

* It was one of the customs of the Omahas to cease wailing at a certain stage in the funeral ceremonies, that the departing friend might not be distressed by the sounds of sorrow, as he left his home behind him,—a custom founded on the same belief as that expressed by this funeral song.

STORY AND SONG OF THE MOTHER'S VOW.

IT was a warm day of early spring on the Upper Missouri, when the subtle joy of awakening life stirs the blood and rouses the fancy. The brown outline of the bare trees was already broken by little leaves that were shaking themselves in the bright sunlight. Flowers were peering through the vivid green of the freshly sprung grass, the birds had come, and the silence of the year had passed. It was a day to enjoy outdoor life, to indulge in hope and happy thoughts. The sky was so blue between the rolling white clouds that one forgot they could ever become portentous of storm. The tents of the Indians, dotted along the banks of the stream, stood like tall white flowers among the trees. Women and children were chatting and calling to each other. Men moved sedately about, busy with preparations for the coming summer days. Young men and maidens were thinking of each other; for the morning song of the lover had been heard, and the signal flash of the mirror* had revealed his watching-place to the dark-eyed girl

_____
* Young men carried small looking-glasses with which they flashed signals.

demurely drawing water for the household in the early dawn.

Unheeding the passage of the hours, I wandered up the narrow valley, noting the fading lines of aboriginal life spread out before me. All at once I became aware that the brightness of the day was overshadowed: a greyish hue, that rapidly deepened, pervaded the scene. Suddenly the wind came over the hills, the birds darted about, and the sound of thunder was heard. Everything was seeking a shelter; and, as I turned in haste, hoping to reach the nearest tent, I saw an old woman emerge from a lodge and in the face of the storm begin to climb the hill, down which the wind swept, laying low the grass and whipping the heads of the flowers. Seemingly unmindful of the storm, on the woman went, her scant garments flapping, and her hair, seamed with grey, tossing about her wrinkled face. The sight was so strange that I paused to watch her, as she climbed on and on, steadfastly breasting the storm. The lightnings flashed around her, and the thunder echoed among the hills as she reached the top. There she stopped and stood, a silhouette against the surging clouds, her hands uplifted, her head thrown back; and between the thunder peals I heard her voice ring out loud and clear in a song,—a song, I doubted not, that carried a message to the mighty storm, in which to her the gods were present. Many years have passed since I witnessed this scene and learned the story of the woman's song. She is now at rest, and let us hope her lifelong sorrow may have turned to joy.

In the early part of the century a Dakota woman fasted and prayed, and Thunder came to her in her vision. To the god she promised to give her firstborn child. When she became a mother, she forgot in her joy that the life of her little one did not belong to her; nor did she recall her fateful vow until one bright spring day, when the clouds gathered and she heard the roll of the thunder,—a sound which summoned all persons consecrated to this god to bring their offerings and to pay their vows. Then she remembered what she had promised; but her heart forbade her to lay the infant, which was smiling in her arms, upon the cloud-swept hill-top. She pressed the baby to her breast, and waited in silence the passing of the god in the storm.

The following spring, when the first thunder pealed, she did not forget her vow; but she could not gather strength to fulfil it.

Another year passed, and again the thunder sounded. Taking the toddling child by the hand, the mother climbed the hill; and, when the top was reached, she placed it on the ground and fled. But the boy scrambled up and ran after her, and his frightened cry stayed her feet. He caught her garments and clung to them; and, although the thunder called, she could not obey. Her vow had been made before she knew the strength of a mother's love.

Gathering the boy in her arms, she hid herself and him from the presence of the god. The storm passed, and the mother and child returned to the lodge; but fear had taken possession of her, and she watched her son with eyes in which terror and love struggled for the mastery.

One day, as the little one played beside a rippling brook, laughing and singing in his glee, suddenly the clouds gathered, the flashing lightning and the crashing thunder sent beast and bird to cover, and drove the mother out to find her child. She heard his voice above the fury of the storm, calling to her. As she neared the brook, a vivid flash blinded her eyes. For a moment she was stunned; but, recovering, she pushed on, only to be appalled

64

by the sight that met her gaze.   Her boy lay dead.
The thunder god had claimed his own.

No other children came to lighten the sorrow of
the lonely woman; and every spring, when the first
thunder sounded, and whenever the storm swept the
land, this stricken woman climbed the hills, and
there, standing alone, facing the black rolling
clouds, she sang her song of sorrow and of fealty.

The words of the song are addressed to the god;
but the music, in its swaying rhythm, suggests the
mother's memory of the days when she soothed her
little child.

The following is a free translation of the Indian
words : —

E dho he!*
Behold!   On their mighty pinions flying,
They come, the gods come once more
Sweeping o'er the land,
Sounding their call to me, to me their own.
Wa-gi-un!† Ye on mighty pinions flying,
Look on me here, me your own,
Thinking on my vow
As ye return once more, Wa-gi-un!

*Sighing vocables.   † Dakota term for the thunder bird.

THE MOTHER'S VOW.

Dakota.

Harmonized by Prof. J. C. Fillmore.

With feeling, dignity and flowing rhythm.

E dho he! Gi-un, gi-un a-gi-ba ha,-don-be

Co-dha, gi-don-be .. a-me, ha-don-be a-me,

Wa-gi-un gi a-me dho he dho-e. Wa-gi-un

THE MOTHER'S VOW.

A LOVE–CALL.

THE native flageolet has proved a trusty friend to many a youth to whom nature had denied the power of expressing in vocal melody his fealty to the maiden of his choice. With its woody tones he rivalled the birds as he sounded his love-call from the hills and made glad the heart of the girl, who, catching the signal, awaited his coming at the spring.

There are many bits of music composed for this little instrument, which, in spite of its inaccuracies of pitch, arising from imperfect construction, are not without hints of beauty.

LOVE CALL.

Omaha.

For the Flageolet.

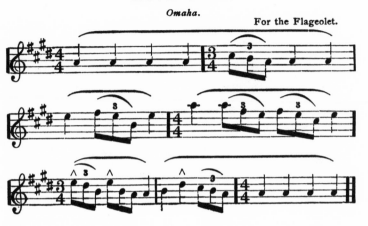

A GAME SONG FROM THE NORTH-WEST COAST.

It is well known that the serious avocations of the fathers often serve as games for the children. So it comes about that in the games of chance we have a survival of the ancient custom of divination. As, according to Indian belief, song was the medium through which man communicated with the mysterious powers, we find all his games of chance accompanied by melodies.

One autumn evening many years ago I was walking along a stretch of the Pacific shore. The westerning moon flooded the water with light, and lit up the edge of the dense forest that formed the background of an Indian village. From one of its great square wooden dwellings came the sound of singing, and the ruddy firelight shone through the cracks of the plank door as I approached.

Entering, I saw that the central fire had just been lighted. The four families, which had each their particular portion of the communal house, had suffered their separate fires to burn to ashes, and had pushed back their various belongings to give more room for the gathering crowd.

A GAME SONG

I lingered at the door, looking on the motley scene: the women and children in the background; the old men in groups, talking over their younger days; the line of men singers, each with his piece of board with which to strike the floor in lieu of a drum; the young men who were to play, ranged in two opposite rows; and others standing about, watching their friends and eager for the game to begin.

When all was ready, the leader of one side held up for a moment in one hand a small piece of bone, then began tossing it secretly from one hand to the other, moving the closed fists rapidly past each other to the rhythm of the song sung by the singers, the opposite side keeping sharp eyes on the moving fists, to be ready, when the signal should be given, to detect, if possible, the hand to which the bone had finally been passed.

Heavy stakes were put up, and there was every sign that song after song would follow each other as the night wore on.

The song which follows is sung when playing a game of chance: —

GAME SONG.

Vancouver's Island.

Transcribed and Harmonized by Prof. J. C. Fillmore.

With strong Rhythm and Abandon.

GAME SONG.

STORY AND SONG OF THE INDIAN COQUET.

In the last century there lived a man who, in his young days, was a desperate coquet. He played havoc with the plans of many a young man, robbing him of the fancy of his sweetheart, and then leaving the maiden all forlorn. His behaviour aroused the anger and jealousy of both sexes, but he seemed as impervious to the contempt of his fellows as he was callous to the woe of his victims. The whole village buzzed with the gossip of his adventures, and every one wondered how he managed to escape punishment.

After the manner of the people, a song was made about him and his career, that has outlasted his vain victories.

It is difficult to convey in concise English the sarcastic humour of the original. The words picture this young man as sitting on a hill, near the village where he lived and achieved so many conquests. The warm summer breeze wafted up to him the hum of the people as they talked, blaming him for his actions. "But why blame me?" says the irresistible youth, stretching himself at full length in the

SONG OF THE INDIAN COQUET.

Omaha.

Harmonized by PROF. J. C. FILLMORE.

sunshine. "It was the gods that made me as I am : blame them, if you will!" And he gave a sigh of satisfaction, "Hi!"

The music carries the story well. The swing of the last six bars suggests his shrug of irresponsibility.

THE OLD MAN'S LOVE-SONG.

EARLY in the century there lived an Omaha Indian, a tall and comely man, gifted with a fine voice and a good memory, and who was greatly admired by the men and women of the tribe. Although genial with every one, he was reserved; and none knew all that had transpired in his life or that occupied his thoughts. He was a prosperous man. His lodge was well supplied, for his skill as a hunter was equal to his valour as a warrior.

Years passed; and here and there a silver thread glistened in his black hair, the furrows deepened in his handsome face, and more and more his thoughts seemed to dwell on the past. One day he was heard singing a love-song of his own composition, and gossip became busy as to what this song might mean. His actions threw no light on the mystery. He was the same kind husband and father, the same diligent provider, and he sought no new companionship. Nevertheless, at every dawn he went upon the hill near his lodge; and, while the morning star hung like a jewel in the east, he sang the melody carrying the words,—

" With the dawn I seek thee ! "

THE OLD MAN'S LOVE SONG.

Omaha.

Harmonized by Prof. J. C. Fillmore.

Solibitum. Flowingly, With feeling.

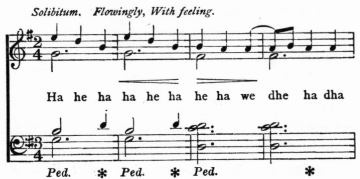

Ha he ha ha he ha he ha we dhe ha dha

Ped.   *   Ped.   *   Ped.   *

e ha dhoe,   Um - ba e - don ha - i - don,

Ped.   *   Ped.   * Ped.   * Ped.   *

hu - wi - ne ha, ho e ho wa dho he dhe, I

Ped.   * Ped.

THE OLD MAN'S LOVE SONG.

The young men caught the tune, and sang it as they wooed the maidens; and the old man smiled as he heard them. "Yes, they are right," he said. "It is a love-song."

He grew to be a very old man, an old man with a love-song, until it was only when the warm days came that he could slowly climb the hill at dawn, and, alone with the breezes and birds, greet the new day with his song, that both kept and revealed his secret,— the secret of a love, like the radiant bow, spanning the whole horizon of his life. At last a time came when his voice was no longer heard.

The tender cadences of his song, fraught with human hope and human feeling, still linger, and to-day awaken echoes across the barriers of time and race.

STORY OF THE WE′–TON SONG.

MANY Indian tribes believed it possible for one person to affect another through the power of the will. This belief gave rise to peculiar customs and to a class of songs called, in the Omaha tongue, We′-ton, composed and sung by women for the sole purpose of exerting this power for the benefit of absent warriors.

Unless the village was attacked, women did not take active part in war. When the men went forth on a long journey to meet the enemy, the women remained at home, attending to domestic duties. Their thoughts, however, were with the absent ones; and, under the incentive of the belief in will power, they would gather in groups at the lodge of the Leader of the war party, and in the hearing of his family would sing a We′-ton song, which should carry strength to the far-away warriors and help them to win the battle.

The words of these songs do not reveal the purpose for which they were sung, it being one of the peculiarities of the Indian never to expatiate upon that which to him is apparent. The gathering of the women at the lodge of the Leader of the war party, the united action in singing a song never used but for one purpose, made any explanatory words seem unnecessary. The distinctive mission of the song was to reach the absent man, who, far from home, was suffering hardship and facing danger. Upon him the singers fixed their thoughts, and to him sent strength by their power of will. The words always referred to the difficulties that confronted the warrior, and promised him success and victory. They were not addressed to any visible audience.

The We'-ton song here given was composed by a Dakota woman.

Many years ago a large party of warriors were out on a dangerous expedition for the purpose of recapturing some property stolen by an implacable enemy. There seemed little hope for their safe return, and great apprehension was felt in many a tent. One evening, as the moon rose, round and clear, over the wide rolling prairie, a group of women moved in single file to the lodge of the Leader of the war party, upon whom rested the responsibility of the expedition.

The tent stood dark against the evening sky, re-

vealing the anxiety within, which had let the blazing fire die to smouldering embers. At the door
the women paused, and across the stillness of the
night they sent forth this song, fraught with their
united determination to compel victory for the
absent men.

"All the tribes shall hear of you," they sang.
"Put forth your strength. Truly this shall come to
pass."

Out of the silent tent emerged the Leader's
wife, bearing in her arms gifts in acknowledgment
of sympathy given and of succour sent.

And, as the women sang, "truly it came to pass."
In due time the men returned triumphant, after
many hair-breadth escapes, with not one of their
number missing.

WE - TON SONG.

Dakota.

Harmonized by Prof. J. C. Fillmore.

With feeling.

E   ya-a   he!   ah   he   dhe   he   dhe

Ped.   * Ped.   *

ah   he   dhe   he   dhe   e - ya   he!   ah   ye

Ped.   * Ped.   * Ped.

dha   he   he   ah   he   dha   he   dhoe,

p

* Ped.   *

WE - TO*N* SONG.

ou - ki - a - ma   dhi   nun - un - ta - ye   wa-

skon - e - gun   ya   he   E   ya   he !

ah   he   dhe   he   he   ah   he   dhe   he   dho.

A PAWNEE LOVE–SONG.

THERE is no dalliance in this Pawnee love-song. It has no words, but the music tells the story, — the insistent call of the lover to the maiden to fly with him, the wide sweep of the prairie, the race for cover, and the dauntless daring that won the girl from rival pursuers.

LOVE SONG.

Pawnee.

Transcribed by E. S. Tracy.

A WARRIOR'S STORY AND SONG.

THE Mi'-ka-thi songs are sung by warriors as they leave the village on their way to battle. They all originate in some personal experience, and both story and song are handed down with care and precision.

A Ponka war party once camped near the enemy. The usual sentinels had been stationed, with special injunctions to be vigilant, that the camp might not be discovered and surprised. Among those assigned to duty as sentinel that night was a young man ambitious to win preferment and honour in the tribe. His career was yet all to make, and he was on the alert for opportunity to distinguish himself.

There was no moon, and only the keenest eye could discern any distant object in the darkness. The silence was unbroken save by the occasional cry of the wolf, the creaking of a cricket, or the rustle of a passing breeze.

The young man, intently on the watch, scanned the country from right to left, searching through the dimness for any moving thing; but all was motionless beneath, while overhead the stars moved slowly through the heavens, as the night wore on.

A WARRIOR'S STORY AND SONG

At a little distance from the watcher was a clump of trees. Upon this he kept a steady eye, only turning now and then to sweep the horizon. Once, as his eye returned to the trees, he beheld a shadow unnoticed before. It moved; and, without waiting to see more, he sped noiselessly as an arrow to wake the Leader and report that he had seen the enemy creeping toward the sleeping warriors.

The Leader, an old and experienced man, made no reply, but rose quickly and silently, and taking his bow in his hand, motioned the sentinel to lead the way.

With rapid, muffled steps, they reached the place where the young man had stood when he had seen the moving shadow. The Leader looked intently in the indicated direction, bent his ear to the ground and listened, then rose and looked again.

A faint gleam of light in the east gave sign of the approach of day, as the Leader stepped cautiously toward the group of trees, followed by the young warrior, whose heart beat high with hope that the time had at last come for him to show his valour and win a war honour. A greyish hue was spreading over the land as they neared the place. The young man's eyes sought among the trees the hidden enemy, but the Leader paused and addressed the youth : —

"Was it here that you saw the enemy?"

"Yes."

"Look on the ground and tell me what you see?"

Surprised at the words, yet obedient, he turned his scrutiny from the trees to the grass upon which they stood, and detected there the traces of the feet of an animal. As he gazed silently at the tracks, absorbed in his thoughts, the dawn came slowly on. The Leader was the first to speak : —

"I had seen a wolf pass here when I was going the rounds of the camp, and when you reported to me I had but just returned to my bed. I arose and came with you, to be quite sure that we had both looked in the same direction and had seen the same thing. A warrior must learn to distinguish a man from a wolf, even in the darkness of midnight."

The youth heard the words in silence. At last he said, "A warrior has much to learn; and it is well if, while he learns, he brings no trouble to his friends." Then, standing beside the veteran Leader, in the light of the coming day, he suddenly broke into song, voicing there on the instant the feeling born of his night's experience.

A WARRIOR'S STORY AND SONG

This story and song he gave to others, that it might be as a voice of warning to young and eager warriors, and help them to guard against a misadventure like his own.

Although the young man in after years became noted in the tribe for his prudence and valour, this story and song of his youth have survived the memory of his later deeds.

The words give the pith of the adventure: "I did not report aright when I went to the Leader and bade him arise. It was a wolf that was moving."

The spirited music breathes the impatient eagerness of youth. The haste and insistence of the young warrior are heard in the phrase where he addresses the "Nu-don hon-ga," or Leader. The song is a great favourite among the young men of several Indian tribes in our country.

MI–KA–THI.

A WARRIOR'S SONG.

Ponka.

Martial. Spirited and lightly.

Hi a ha ha ha a he a -

we dho he . . e hu he a he

dhe ya a ho e dho he . . e hu

e a - he ya a ha e dho he . . he . .

MI-KA-THI.

dho-e. Nu-don hon-ga ni - a - shi-ga bi-e he mia ka

non-zhi-a he . . . e Mi - ka - thi - a -

ma ha dhea a - me dho he . . . e Hon-

ga dhe - te non zhin - ge dho he . . . e.

THE MOCKING–BIRD'S SONG.

THIS little song of springtime was noted from the singing of a Tigua girl of the pueblo of Isleta, N. M., by my honoured and lamented friend and co-worker, Professor John Comfort Fillmore. It tells the story of the semi-arid region where it was born.

> Rain, people, rain!
> The rain is all around us.
> It is going to come pouring down,
> And the summer will be fair to see,
> The mocking-bird has said so.

MOCKING BIRD SONG.

Tigua.

Transcribed and harmonized
by PROF. JOHN COMFORT FILLMORE.

Hla - chi dai - nin, hla - chi dai - nin,

i-beh ma kun whi ni weh, da win gu ba hin ah.

Ah hlun hla hlue i hi ei - ah whi no ei - ah whi no

i-ah ei-ah hi-ah hin ni ni ah. Tur

wey u tur p'hoa whe na he de a na lhen h'li

he pun hi ni ni ah Li u yu sa na

a a . . a ya he wa a

hi ni ni a hi ni ni a ni a a ha i hi.

A SONG OF THE GHOST DANCE.

THERE are few more pathetic sights than that of an Indian ghost dance, — pathetic in itself, not to consider the gloomy background of fear inspired by it in the minds of so many of our own race who have so widely misunderstood its meaning. The ceremony is but an appeal to the unseen world to come near and to comfort those who have been overtaken in the land of their fathers by conditions both strange and incomprehensible.

The ghost or spirit dance is a modified survival of several ancient ceremonies, blended into one and touched here and there with ideas borrowed from our own race.

In the hypnotic vision which follows the monotonous dance, the landscape of his former days, untouched by the white man, appears to the "controlled" Indian: the streams wander through unbroken prairie; no roadways, no fields of wheat, intrude upon the broad stretches of native grasses; the vanished herds of buffalo come back to their grazing-grounds; the deer and the antelope, the wolf and the bear, are again in the land; and the eagles look down on the Indian villages, where are to be

96

A SONG OF THE GHOST DANCE

seen the faces of old friends returned from the spirit
realm. These are the scenes which come to the
homesick Indian, who is stranded in his native
land, his ears filled with foreign sounds, his old
activities gone, and his hands unskilled and unable
to take up new ones.

The ghost dance is the cry of a forsaken people,
forsaken by the gods in which they once trusted,—
a people bewildered by the complexity of the new
path they must follow, misunderstood by and mis-
understanding the race with whom they are forced
to live. In this brief ceremony of the ghost dance
the Indians seek to close their eyes to an unwel-
come reality, and to live in the fanciful vision of
an irrecoverable past.

This song was given me by a ghost dancer, a
leader in the Arapaho tribe. Before he sang, he
explained to me the ceremony, its peaceful character, and, all unconsciously, made apparent its expression of a pathetic longing for a life that can
never return. Standing before the graphophone, he
offered an earnest prayer, then, with his companions,
sang this song.

The simple pathos of the words cannot be repro-

GHOST DANCE SONG.

Arapaho.

GHOST DANCE SONG

duced in English. They carry a meaning beneath their literal sense that appeals like the cry of a child.

> Father, have pity upon me!
> I am weeping from hunger (of the spirit):
> There is nothing here to satisfy me!

The music tells the story of the cry. Its cadences are antiphonal, as between the two worlds.

SACRED SONGS OF PEACE.

WHEN the white race first visited the Indians in the Mississippi valley, they found among them a ceremony common to a large number of tribes; and it was observed that, whenever the symbolic objects peculiar to this ceremony were displayed, they were treated with profound respect.

These sacred objects were two perforated sticks, like pipe stems, one painted blue to represent the sky, and the other green to typify the earth; and among their bright-coloured decorations were the plumages of particular birds and wing-like pendants of eagle feathers. They symbolised the heavens and the earth and the mysterious power that permeates all nature. In their presence the Indians were taught that they should care for their children, think of the future welfare of the people, put aside personal grievances, repress anger and warlike emotions, and be like kindred, at peace with one another. Different names were given to these peculiar objects by the different tribes; and they were classed by our early travellers with the "calumets," or pipes of peace, although they were not pipes, for they had no bowl and could not be smoked.

It was due to the presence of one of these so-called "calumets" in Marquette's frail canoe that made possible his peaceful descent of the Mississippi River on his voyage of discovery. He writes that the "calumet is the most mysterious thing in the world. The sceptres of our kings are not so much respected; . . . for one with this calumet may venture among his enemies, and in the hottest battles they lay down their arms before this sacred pipe."

The "calumet" ceremony has, therefore, an historic interest for us, apart from its revelation of the religious beliefs and social ideals of the Indian. To explain the symbolism, the teachings, and the observances which make up this complex rite would fill a volume; but, that something of the dignity and beauty of the thoughts expressed in it may be known, two of its numerous songs are here given.

To understand the significance of these songs, it should be known that two distinct groups or parties were indispensable to the performance of the ceremony; namely, they who brought the "calumets" and they who received them. As it was imperative that there should be no blood relationship between these two parties, they always belonged to different tribes or to two distinct kinship groups within the tribe. The party bringing the "calumets" was called "the father," while those receiving them were "the children." These terms refer to the tie about to be formed between the two unrelated parties by means of this sacred ceremony. This tie was esteemed more honourable and binding than the natural bond of father and son.

The ceremony generally took place in a circular dwelling known as an "earth lodge." The occasion drew together a large concourse of people,— men, women, and children; and the gay costumes, the glinting of ornaments, the picturesque groups, and the happy, smiling faces of old and young made a scene full of colour and motion. Many times I have witnessed this ceremony and joined in its beautiful chorals, led by the bearers, who swayed the "calumets" to the rhythm of the song, wafting over the heads of the people the blessing of peace.

The following choral was sung immediately after the "calumets" had been ceremonially taken from their resting-place, with movements that simulated the eagle rising from its nest. The bearers then faced the people, seated on the ground against the wall of the lodge, and with slow rhythmic steps moved around the circle, waving the "calumets" over the heads of the multitude. As the "calumets" passed slowly by, the people took up the choral, until at last the great lodge resounded with its majestic cadences. The leaping flames from the central fire lit up the faces of the hundreds of men and women; while the swaying feathers of the "calumets" cast great wing-like shadows on the glistening roof, and seemed to make real the symbolic presence of the mighty eagle himself, circling over the people as he sped on his mission, bearing the benediction of good will among men.

Once, at the close of this song, an old Indian turned to me and said, "The 'calumets' are of God."

The words of this choral refer to the blessing of peace given to "the fathers" in ancient days, and now brought by the symbolic "calumets" to "the children."

> Down through the ages vast,
> On wings strong and true,
> From great Wa-kon'-da comes
> Good will unto you,—
> Peace, that shall here remain.

CHORAL.

Omaha.

Harmonized by Prof. J. C. Fillmore.

After the bearers, or "the fathers," had ceremonially borne the "calumets" four times around the lodge, singing as they went and waving the blessing of peace and fellowship over the heads of "the children," they paused as they reached a consecrated place at the back of the lodge, facing the entrance to the east. Here the ground had been specially prepared, and a wildcat skin spread upon it for the reception of the "calumets." Over this skin, which had its symbolic meaning, the bearers waved the "calumets," imitating the movements of the eagle, sweeping lower and lower, rising and circling again, and then dropping lightly upon its nest.

The song is one of those sung to accompany the movements of the "calumets" as they are thus lowered to rest. The words refer to the search of "the fathers" for "the children," to bring them peace, as the eagle soars abroad and returns to its nest.

> Far above the earth he soars,
> Circling the clear sky,
> Flying over forests dim,
> Peering in shadows,
> Seeking far and wide his child,
> To give him peace.

THE GIFT OF PEACE.

Otoe.

Harmonized by Prof. J. C. Fillmore.

With feeling. Lightly and smoothly.

Zhin-ga dha-we dho   dho we   he   ho-i

Tremolo of the drum.

ne Zhin-ga dha-we dho   dho we . .   he

ho-i - ne Zhin-ga dha we dho dho we ha je dha we.

COMFORTING THE CHILD.

THE three following songs have a common motive, and are parts of one ceremonial action; but the motive is treated differently in each song, so as to conform to the movements of the ceremony.* An unconscious art is here shown, which is interesting as a bit of musical archæology. During the "calumet" ceremony among the Pawnees, if a child cried and would not be comforted, its parents were permitted to appeal to the "calumets" for help.

The fan-shaped pendant of one of these "calumets" was made of the feathers of the golden eagle. This bird in the ceremony was called Kawas, and symbolised the peaceful and conserving power, the giver and preserver of life, the parent of all things. It was to the priestly bearer of this particular "calumet" that the parents appealed. On receiving the appeal, the priest and his assistants arose, and, standing beside "the holy place,"—the consecrated space where the "calumets" were laid at ceremonial rest,—they sang this song, thus passing on to Kawas the appeal of the parents.

* These songs were never before noted, and have hitherto been sealed from the knowledge of the white race. They were given and explained by a priest of the rite, through Mr. James R. Murie.

KAWAS, THY BABY IS CRYING.

Pawnee.

Transcribed from Graphophone record
and Harmonized by E. S. TRACY.

Swinging rhythm.

INTRO.

Ho   o Ka - was   ta   wha-ka ra-tsa we   Ka -

Ped.   Ped.   Ped.

was   ta . .   wha-ka ra - tsa . . we

Ah   he - wi!   wha-ka ra-tsa   we,   Ka -

Ped.   Ped.   Ped.

- - was   ta . .   wha-ka - ra   tsa . . we.

INDIAN STORY AND SONG

The words are in the nature of a prayer, the music has the swing of a lullaby.

> Kawas, thy baby is crying!
> Grieving sore, wailing, and weeping.
> Aye, forsooth! wailing and weeping,
> Kawas, thy baby is crying!

Then the bearers took up the "calumets" and moved with slow rhythmic steps toward the crying child, singing as they went and swaying the sacred symbols to the measure of this song. Its meaning was explained to me as follows:—

"Hah-ars (a contraction of the word meaning father) signifies Ti-ra'-wa, the power that animates all things, all animals, all men, the heavens, and the earth. Ti-ra'-wa is represented by the Hako (the 'calumets'), and it is this power which now approaches to console the child."

In the music one hears the coming of Ti-ra'-wa in the footsteps of his creatures, both great and small.

> Thy father is coming,
> E'en now he is near thee;
> Cry no more: the mighty one,
> Thy father, is coming!

THY FATHER IS COMING.

Pawnee.

Transcribed from Graphophone record and
Harmonized by E. S. TRACY.

Smoothly but with marked rhythm.

Upon reaching the child, the golden eagle "calu-met" was gently swayed above it, while in the background the other "calumet" was waved to ward off disturbing influences, and the priests sang this song. It is said that on hearing it "the child always looks up and ceases its crying."

The caressing, almost playful rythm of the music twines about the deep religious feeling expressed in the words, like the arms of an infant about the neck of its thoughtful, reverent parent.

> Lift thine eyes, 'tis the gods who come near,
> Bringing thee joy, release from all pain.
> Sending sorrow and sighing
> Far from the child, Ti-ra'-wa makes fain.
>
> Ah, you look! Surely, you know who comes,
> Claiming you his and bidding you rise,
> Blithely smiling and happy,
> Child of Ti-ra'-wa, Lord of the skies!

LOOK UP!

Pawnee.

Transcribed from Graphophone record, and
Harmonized by E. S. TRACY.

Swinging rhythm. Lightly.

Ho . . Ha! Is - te wa - ta si wi - ta ha,

. . . Ha! Is - te wa - ta si . . wi - ta

. . ha . . Hah - ars . . hi . . re wa -

ha - ki, Ha! Is - te wa - ta si . . wi - ta ha.

MUSIC IN INDIAN LIFE.

Music enveloped the Indian's individual and social life like an atmosphere. There was no important personal experience where it did not bear a part, nor any ceremonial where it was not essential to the expression of religious feeling. The songs of a tribe were coextensive with the life of the people.

This universal use of music was because of the belief that it was a medium of communication between man and the unseen. The invisible voice could reach the invisible power that permeates all nature, animating all natural forms. As success depended upon help from this mysterious power, in every avocation, in every undertaking, and in every ceremonial, the Indian appealed to this power through song. When a man went forth to hunt, that he might secure food and clothing for his family, he sang songs to insure the assistance of the unseen power in capturing the game. In like manner, when he confronted danger and death, he sang that strength might be given him to meet his fate unflinchingly. In gathering the healing herbs and in administering them, song brought the required efficacy. When he planted, he sang, in order that the seed might fructify and the harvest follow. In his sports, in his games, when he wooed and when he mourned, song alike gave zest to pleasure and brought solace to his suffering. In fact, the Indian sang in every experience of life from his cradle to his grave.

It would be a mistake to fancy that songs floated indiscriminately about among the Indians, and could be picked up here and there by any chance observer. Every song had originally its owner. It belonged either to a society, secular or religious, to a certain clan or political organization, to a particular rite or ceremony, or to some individual.

Religious songs were known only to the priesthood; and, as music constituted a medium between man and the unseen powers which controlled his life, literal accuracy was important, otherwise the path between the god and the man would not be straight, and the appeal would miscarry.

In every tribe there were societies having a definite membership, with initiatory rites and reciprocal duties. Each society had its peculiar songs; and there were officials chosen from among the members because of their good voices and retentive memories, to lead the singing and to transmit with accuracy the stories and songs of the society, which frequently preserved bits of tribal history. Fines were imposed upon any member who sang incorrectly, while ridicule always and everywhere followed a faulty rendering of a song.

The right to sing a song which belonged to an individual could be purchased, the person buying the song being taught it by its owner.

These beliefs and customs among the Indians have made it possible to preserve their songs without change from one generation to another. Many curious and interesting proofs of accuracy of transmittal have come to my knowledge during the past twenty years, while studying these primitive melodies.

Indian singing was always in unison; and, as the natural soprano, contralto, tenor, and bass moved along in octaves, the different qualities of tone in the voices brought out the overtones and produced harmonic effects. When listening to chorals sung by two or three hundred voices, as I have many times heard them in ceremonials, it has been difficult to realise that all were singing in unison.

Close and continued observation has revealed that

the Indian, when he sings, is not concerned with
the making of a musical presentation to his audience. He is simply pouring out his feelings,
regardless of artistic effects. To him music is sub-
jective: it is the vehicle of communication between
him and the object of his desire.

Certain peculiarities in the Indian's mode of
singing make it difficult for one of our race to in-
telligently hear their songs or to truthfully tran-
scribe them.

There is no uniform key for any given song, for
the Indians have no mechanical device for determin-
ing pitch to create a standard by which to train the
ear. This, however, does not affect the song; for,
whatever the starting note, the intervals bear the
same relation to each other, so that the melody
itself suffers no change with the change of pitch.

Again, the continual slurring of the voice from
one tone to another produces upon us the impression
of out-of-tune singing. Then, the custom of singing out of doors, to the accompaniment of the drum,
and against the various noises of the camp, and the
ever-restless wind, tending to strain the voice and
robbing it of sweetness, increases the difficulty of
distinguishing the music concealed within the

noise,— a difficulty still further aggravated by the habit of pulsating the voice, creating a rhythm within the rhythm of the song.

Emotion also affects the rendering of Indian music. This is especially noticeable in solos, as love-songs, where the singer quite unconsciously varies from a quarter to a whole tone from the true pitch. On the contrary, emphasis sharps the tone. If, however, these peculiarities are imitated to him, the Indian immediately detects, and declares them to be wrong, thus betraying his unconsciousness of his own inaccuracies in endeavouring to strike a plain diatonic interval.

Our difficulty in hearing the music of the Indian is equalled by the trouble he has with our instruments. His attention is engaged by the mechanism. He hears the thud of the hammer, "the drum inside" the piano, the twanging of the metal strings, and the abrupt, disconnected tones. Until he is able to ignore these noises he cannot recognise the most familiar tune. Even then, if his songs are played as an unsupported aria, they are unsatisfactory to him. His ear misses something it heard in the unison singing of his people, and which the addition of a simple harmonic accompaniment supplies, making the melody, as he says, "sound natural." The discovery of the Indian's preference in the rendition of his songs upon the piano led to many experiments, in which Professor Fillmore took part, and that brought to light many interesting facts. Among these facts may be mentioned the complexity of rythms, one played against the other; the modulation implied in some of the melodies; the preference for a major chord in closing a minor song; and the use of certain harmonic relations which have been deemed peculiar to the modern romantic school.

As these melodies are the spontaneous utterances of a people without any theory of music or even a musical notation, they throw light upon the structure, development, and freedom of natural expression in music.

THE RELATION OF STORY AND SONG.

THE rise of our music and poetry is lost in an irrevocable past; but, as the operation of psychical laws is universal, it may be that some of the influences that have been operative in the growth of these arts can be discovered through the study of native American story and song, born of a race living in a state of culture antecedent to that in which our earliest literature and music flourished.

Within a generation diligent search has begun among some of the Indian tribes, to ascertain, through a sympathetic study of rites, ceremonies, and customs, what were the red man's ideals, what his beliefs, and what his actual attainments. Already this labour is bearing fruit. Scholars are recognising that the aboriginal conditions on this continent throw light on the slow development of human society and its institutions; and the time seems not distant when students of man's culture will turn hither for evidence needed to fill gaps or to explain phases in the development of art,—art in form, in colour, and in melody,—for, it has been well said, America is the "fossil bed" where are preserved stages of progress unrecorded in written history.

THE RELATION OF STORY AND SONG

In Indian story and song we come upon a time where poetry is not yet differentiated from story and story not yet set free from song. We note that the song clasps the story as a part of its being, and the story itself is not fully told without the cadence of the song. Yet in even the most primitive examples a line of demarcation can be discerned; and when this line has deepened, and differentiation has begun, we are able to trace the formative influence exerted by story upon song and by song upon story, and can observe what appear to be the beginnings of musical and poetical structure.

The brevity of Indian songs at once arrests attention. They begin without introduction, almost abruptly, breaking out upon us as though surcharged. This peculiarity arises from the relation of the song to the story. The story is always founded upon a dramatic circumstance, in which at some point the emotion is forced to find a means of expression beyond the limitation of words alone; and the song is the result. This dramatic circumstance may be a danger confronted or averted, a valorous deed achieved or a difficulty surmounted, a religious experience or an ardent craving for supernatural aid. The Omaha tribal prayer will serve as an illustration, where the cry to Wa-kon-da is the climatic voicing of the youth's desire in the midst of his weary vigil and fasting. His long preparation for the rite, the solitude of his surroundings, the suffering of mind and body as alone he faces nature and the supernatural,—all these conditions make the story, and, to the Indian, form the true setting of the song.

The motive of a song and its distinctive rhythm were determined by the emotion evoked by the dramatic circumstance. The simplest resultant of this directive emotion in music is a pulsating rhythm on a single tone. Such songs are not random shoutings, but have a definite meaning for those who sing and for those who listen, as in this Navaho ritual song.

From this extremely simple expression the growth of the musical motive can be traced in these Indian songs through the use of two or more tones up to the employment of the full complement of the octave.*

* A careful analysis of hundreds of aboriginal songs, gathered from the arctic seas to the tropics, shows that in every instance the line taken by these tones is a

A PRAYER FOR RAIN.

Mexico. Tarahumare.

From DR. CARL LUMHOLTZ.

SONG.

British Columbia. Kwakiutl.

PROF. J. C. FILLMORE.

chord-line where the tones are harmonically related to each other. Out of these related tones the untutored savage has built his simple melodies. The demonstration of the interesting fact that "the line of least resistance" in music is a harmonic line was made by my late associate, Professor John Comfort Fillmore.

123

The creation of that which we know as musical form seems also to be due to the influence of story upon song. We have already noted how the directive emotion started the distinctive rythm and determined the order of the related tones, and so constructed the motive or theme. But neither the rythm nor the simple motive could express the *movement* of the dramatic story: hence we find this expressed by the repetition, modification, and variation of the motive, the growth of the phrase, the formation of the clause, and the grouping of clauses into a period, — in fact, the outline of the form upon which all our culture music is built. Culture music, however, shows an intellectual control of emotion, a power of musical thinking, the enlarging and embellishing of musical form, — a form, nevertheless, which we find outlined, more or less clearly, in the songs of the untutored red man. The difference between these spontaneous Indian melodies and the compositions of the modern masters would seem to be not one of kind, but one of degree.

As these songs are from a race practically without musical instruments, — for the drum and rattle were used only to accentuate rythm, — they are representative of the period when the human voice was

the sole means of musical expression,— a period
which antedated the invention of instruments by an
immeasurable time.   They prove, therefore, that
musical form was not developed, as has sometimes
been stated, by the use of instruments, but that it
took its rise in a mental necessity similar to that
which gave structure to language.

The influence of song upon story is seen in the
attempt to bend prose to a poetic form.

Many Indian songs have no words at all, vocables
only being used to float the voice.   On classifying
these wordless songs, we discover that those which
are expressive of the gentle emotions have flowing,
breathing vocables, but, where warlike feelings
dominate the song, the vocables are aspirate and
explosive.   In this determinate use of vocables we
happen upon what seems to represent the most primitive attempt yet discovered to give intellectual
definition in verbal form to an emotion voiced in
rythm and melody.

In songs where words are employed, we also find
vocables which are in accord with the spirit of the
song, used to make the words conform to the musical phrase.   These vocables are either appended
to the word or else inserted between its syllables,

to give length or added euphony. We also note a desire for rhyming, since vocables similar in sound frequently occur at the end of each musical phrase.

It would lead into too many details to present the various devices discernible in this aboriginal material by which the Indian sought euphony and measure. Nor can it be easily illustrated how words of many different languages were bent by elisions or stretched by vocables, that they might conform to the musical phrase. There is abundant evidence that the ear, accustomed to the pleasure of the rythmic cadence of the song, was beginning to demand a corresponding metrical use of words in expressing the poetic thought involved in the dramatic story which gave birth to the music.

The art of poetry is here in its infancy, giving even less sign of its future development than music, which had already acquired the outline of that form which has since crystallised into the art of music. Notwithstanding, we find that words were chosen for their descriptive power, and that they were made rythmical to fit the melody. Like the swelling buds on the bare branch, which hint the approach of summer's wealth, so these little vocables and rythmic devices whisper the coming of the poets.